I AM DEBORAH:
Leadership has no gender

DR. JUANITA JULIA

TRILOGY

Trilogy Christian Publishers

A Wholly Owned Subsidiary of Trinity Broadcasting Network

2442 Michelle Drive

Tustin, CA 92780

For information, address Trilogy Christian Publishing

Rights Department, 2442 Michelle Drive, Tustin, Ca 92780.

Trilogy Christian Publishing/ TBN and colophon are trademarks of Trinity Broadcasting Network.

For information about special discounts for bulk purchases, please contact Trilogy Christian Publishing.

10 9 8 7 6 5 4 3 2 1

Library of Congress Cataloging-in-Publication Data is available.

ISBN 979-8-89041-270-6

ISBN 979-8-89041-271-3 (ebook)

I AM DEBORAH:
Leadership has no gender

DEDICATION

This book is dedicated to every woman who feels called to greatness but has not moved toward greatness. Time waits for no one, so feel great but, more importantly, be great! You got this girl!

FORWARD

"Women belong in all places where decisions
are being made. It shouldn't be that women are
the exception."

- Ruth Bader Ginsburg[1].

This quote was the best sentiment that I could express when
it came to the thoughts of this amazing book written by my sister
Dr. Juanita Julia. Her creative mind to minister and empower the
mindset of women will provoke its readers to inhale possibility
and exhale strategy. The way she brought Deborah's life to life was
like I was sitting in a coffee shop having a conversation with her;
I was having an experience about her life journey. Dr. Julia speaks
to the leader that we all possess, knowingly and unknowingly;
the staff-led anchor in your goals, dreams, and aspirations will be
broken while walking through the pages of this book.

The way she compartmentalizes the many hats of a woman is
defining; she does not rob any capacity of who we are as women.
Sisters, you need this book as a tool, as a resource to assist you in
your leadership abilities. She reveals the tenderness, boss woman,
the trailblazer, and the thinking tank of a woman. In this book,
I see the wisdom of God navigating her mind, speaking through
her soul, and releasing her spirit to write prophetically, giving
God's best a staple in time. Women, we have a voice; we are a
movement. We are game changers and power players, and this is
what this book projects. One of my many best statements is that
there are three types of people in the book of Judges:

People who love God
People who pretend to love God
People who don't love God

How befitting are those points to the culture of today? As we see the depth of transition happening before our eyes, these points give us a mental reprieve in handling the people we serve daily.

"Deborah the Bee" can be sweet yet strong, which is this masterpiece's undertone.

Sis, you did this! Thank you for putting in the work to bring Deborah to life and allowing us to breathe and become. Thank you for releasing us women to thrive strong and finish. Thank you for ministering and giving the necessary insights to master, sustain, and remain solid in a changing world. Thank you for allowing us to stay great and be okay with being a voice in our culture.

Dr. Ane Mercer

Author, Founder of Ane Mercer
Ministries, CEO of Black Dress White Pearl,
Saved Girls Rock and Certified Transformation Coach

ACKNOWLEDGMENTS

I'd like to acknowledge a few people that have greatly impacted my life. I would not be me without you. So, thank you!

My children Tyler, Madisyn, and Marshall Thomas: Well, let's just say we have grown up together. The best part of my life is seeing you happy and seeing you flourish. I love you all very much.

My spiritual parents, Elder Virgil and Mother Vieta Foster, a.k.a Brother and Sister V.

My pastor, Dr. Robert E. Fowler Sr. (RIP), you told me I was smart at 26 years old and guess what it turns out you were right!

My friend, and the person who sowed the first seeds toward the completion of this book, Dr. Kevin James.

The church family who helped me discover that I was completely built for this, Christ the King Christian Fellowship. My days with you will forever be in my memory. Thanks for six great years.

My Mother, Juanita E. Dalton (RIP), I love you and miss you every day.

My Sister, Dineen McSwain, thanks for all the love and support you've shown me my entire life.

My twin brother, Juan Calvin, you've been my best friend literally from birth. Thanks for just letting me be Cookie and just a friendly reminder, I was born first.

To Bobby Boucher, thank you for being my Lappidoth.

And last but not least, to the God of all creation whom I've failed. Whose direction I've not followed at times in my walk.

Whom I've out right refused His guidance. Whom I haven't always trusted. BUT who loves me, has cared for me, who has inspired me, who has made ways for me that I could not make for myself, it's to You I owe everything. I've been following You my entire life (maybe not like I should have) but even when broken, beat down, depressed, fearful, unmotivated I never gave up on You and it's because You've never gave up on me. I love You and thank You for everything. This book is dedicated especially to You, the one that is, the one that was, and the one that is yet to come. Thank You! I owe you my life.

TABLE OF CONTENTS

Dedication 5

Forward.. 7

Acknowledgments 9

Introduction.. 13

Chapter 1 - Deborah, The Wife & Mother...................... 15

Chapter 2 - Deborah the Devoted Leader......................... 23

Chapter 3 - Deborah the Beautiful 31

Chapter 4 - Deborah the Woke 41

Chapter 5 - Deborah and Lappidoth 47

Chapter 6 - Deborah the Chain Breaker........................... 53

Chapter 7 - Deborah for such a time 61

Chapter 8 - Deborah and the Apostle Paul 69

Chapter 9 - Deborah and Jael... 79

Chapter 10 - Deborah and you....................................... 85

Endnotes 91

INTRODUCTION

How do you summarize who Deborah of the Bible was? She was not just a warrior, but she was a worshipper. She wasn't just a songstress; she was sincere. She wasn't just a judge; she was a jewel. She wasn't just graceful; she had grit. She was the type of woman, in one way or another, that all Christian women should try and emulate. Deborah was a prophetess, judge, and priestess, she was courageous, faithful, action oriented, and an anointed singer. She is the only female judge and one of two people to hold the title of prophet and judge. Her name is translated in the Hebrew as "bee." She is a strong woman of faith and spiritual leader to both males and females. She is trusted by the Israelites because of her reliability and tenacity. Typically, when we think of a prophet we think of men. It is uncommon for a woman to be known for prophetic work, especially in the days of the Bible. So, this must mean that Deborah was special. I do believe that women hold a special place in God's sight, but it was very uncommon for a woman to play any significant role in most stories of the Bible. Deborah was raised up because of the "R" Cycle.

- ☉ **Rebellion**- The Israelites did evil in the sight of the Lord
- ☉ **Retribution**- God was angry about their disobedience and defiance
- ☉ **Repentance**- The Israelites asked for forgiveness
- ☉ **Restoration**- God forgave them

God raised Deborah up for that season and He allowed her God-given leadership ability to take center court. Isn't it amazing how God can make what seems to be an awful situation and turn it into something great? God literally raised this woman up to be great. She is the only female judge recorded in the Bible which means she holds a special place in Jewish and Christian history. So, what happened that pushed Deborah into greatness? It was the state that Israel was in, but it was also her willingness to do something about it. Greatness is not just seeing something but greatness requires that we do something about what we see. Deborah saw the oppression of the Israelites and was frustrated by it and gave leadership to it with the Lord's leading.

According to the book of Judges, King Jabin was a ruthless, merciless oppressive king who terrorized the Israelites for 20 years. Deborah was frustrated with the unjust and barbaric treatment of the Israelites, so she used her gift to free them and give God the glory in the process. To be an effective leader, you must not only see oppression, but you must act on behalf of the oppressed. I call it "speaking truth to power no matter the cost." You must get fed up with the status quo and do something about it. Where would we be without the MLK's of the world, the Abraham Lincoln's of the world? We'd be stuck allowing a certain class of people to be mishandled simply because they have a different skin color. We need leaders that will stand up to oppression even if the oppression doesn't directly impact them. The oppression by the hands of King Jabin was so bad that the Israelites could not defend themselves. They were oppressed and left with no hope and no means to get out of the situation they were in (read Judges 5:8). The Bible says, "And we know that in all things God works for the good of those who love him, who have been called according to his purposes" (Romans 8:28). The Israelites loved God and we know that they were His chosen people, so let's take this journey together and watch how He turns their mess into a miracle while using one woman to bring them out of their oppressive state with skill, class, and leadership.

CHAPTER 1

Deborah, The Wife & Mother

Deborah Is On the Short List.

Before we get into Deborah as a wife and a mother I first want to start with her call. We'll deep dive into her call later in this book but there are a few things I want you to understand about her call and why it was special, but I also want to show you about Jesus and His view of women in ministry. I'm sure you've figured out that there is a short list of women using their prophetic gifts in the Bible. Deborah was one of a few women who was given the title prophetess. Here are the names of other women in the Bible who were prophetesses as well:

- Miriam
- Holda
- Ana

These were the only women who were called by name. There are others, like Philips' daughters, but these four women were named specifically. There's a lot I can say about women and the church, but that may be another book for another day. What I will say is Jesus loved women. They were important to Him. Jesus healed women, defended woman, and depended upon women. One thing I love about Jesus is He is always rooting for the underdog. In first-century Israel women were not trusted, undervalued, and underrated, yet Jesus chooses women to be the first to spread the good news of the gospel. Why would Jesus do that? I believe He did this to show how much He loved women and how He had confidence in their ability. While many mistrusted, undervalued, and underrated women, Jesus valued, trusted, and believed that they were the preachers of the hour as it relates to the introduction of the good news that would change the world. They carried the good news to the men who would then go and change the world. So, why aren't there more women preaching, teaching, and leading in the Bible? I believe it is because Jesus knew His audience. He knew that He could trust women with this powerful message, but He also knew (at least at that time) many would not receive them simply because of their gender. One thing I know for sure concerning women and their leadership role, specifically preaching the gospel, is Jesus believed, permitted, and used women in ministry roles, even those roles that were typically reserved for men. In later chapters I want to deep dive into the scriptures that seem to be the most challenging for people to understand and take those principles and apply them to the world we are in currently, but for now let's look at Deborah the mother.

Deborah the Mother

Deborah, in the book of Judges, refers to herself as the mother to Israel. We don't know if Deborah had biological children, but we know she was a mother type to Israel. When I think about a mother, I think of a woman who is loving, concerned, wise, and female. You may be thinking that of course she is female, but that's important to note because that could be why God chose Deborah. Specifically because she was a female. I believe in that time in Israel's history they needed balance. Women tend to be balanced. We can be soft but hard, simple and complicated, gentle but stern. Women are balanced. Israel needed someone like Deborah who seemed to have a sword in one hand and a song in the other. Her name means bee. She can be sweet like honey but sting like a bee if you come for her. Just like any mother who thinks her children are being bullied will stand against anybody and everybody to defend her children. We see Deborah no different than Mom's all over the world. We love, defend, forgive, and encourage our children to be everything God has called them to be. Deborah was all those things for the people of Israel.

She Was a Wife

Just because a woman is moving in her gifts does not negate that her first ministry starts at home. Women were created to be a helper to their husbands. Notice I said help, not slave nor subordinate. A woman is to come alongside her husband and help him. Unfortunately, we don't know how Deborah balanced ministry and marriage, but we do know she was married to a man named Lapidoth. Here's the thing, that's all we know. We don't hear anything else about him other than he was married to Deborah. In a later chapter I want to give a unique insight on why I believe that is, but for now let's continue. God has a certain structure for marriage. For those who may need a crash course on the structure of a healthy Christian marriage, let me give it to you before we move on with the book. According to Genesis 2:20 Eve was made for the purpose of helping Adam. A healthy marriage understands the principle of a wife helping her husband. When a woman understands and practices this principle, she is an example of the Holy Spirit at work in her marriage.

I was created for the purpose of helping Mike.

What does the Holy Spirit do for us?

#1 The Holy Spirit gives us *wisdom*

I keep asking that the God of our Lord and Savior Jesus Christ, the glorious Father, may give you the Spirit of wisdom and revelation, so that you may know him better. 1 Corinthians 1:17

A wife should speak wisdom to her husband. I'm reminded of the story in the book of 1 Samuel 25. It's the story of Abigail, her husband Nabel and King David. When you get an opportunity read the entire chapter, but to sum the story up it's a story of a woman who not only spoke with wisdom, but she moved with wisdom. I'm hoping you understand that speaking wise and moving wise are two completely different things. Nabel was a foolish, selfish, and mean man. He was a rich man with thousands of livestock at his disposal. David and his troops were on the run from King Saul and were close to Nabel's flock during shearing season. David and his men were running low on supplies, so David sent some of his men to request help from Nabel. Nabel sent word back to David via his men and basically said "No way am I sending anything back to you." David's reaction was swift and forceful. He told his men to strap on their swords because it's about to go down. Abagail got word of what was going on and began to act quickly on her husband's behalf. She prepared food and livestock and she and her servants gave it to David and his men. This act made David hold his troops back from killing Nabel and had them return back to their camp. This is the picture of a wife who God honors. A wife understands the shortcomings of her husband and does not let his shortcomings stop her from doing what is right by her husband and what is right by God.

#2 The Holy Spirit has our best interest at heart

Wives, in the same way submit yourselves to your own husbands so that, if any of them do not believe the word, they may be won over without words by the behavior of their wives, ² when they see the purity and reverence of your lives. ³ Your beauty should not come from outward adornment, such as elaborate hairstyles and the wearing of gold jewelry or fine clothes. ⁴ Rather, it should be that of your inner self, the unfading beauty of a gentle and quiet spirit, which is of great worth in God's sight. ⁵ For this is the way the holy women of the past who put their hope in God used to adorn themselves. They submitted themselves to their own husbands, ⁶ like Sarah, who obeyed Abraham and called him her lord. You are her daughters if you do what is right and do not give way to fear.

⁷ Husbands, in the same way be considerate as you live with your wives, and treat them with respect as the weaker partner and as heirs with you of the gracious gift of life, so that nothing will hinder your prayers.

1 Peter 3:1-7

A wife should have her husband's best interest at heart. She is supposed to walk with a spiritual stance that her husband will believe. I want to stop there. 1 Peter 3:1-7 is not just for the wife who has an unbelieving husband, but this scripture should apply to the wife who has a saved husband. How do we apply this scripture to husbands that are already saved when the scripture is clearly talking about a saved wife and an unbelieving husband? It applies to believing (saved) husbands because the saved wife should help her saved husband to believe in her. Believe that she has his best interest at heart. That she's going to walk in the ways of the Lord with a gentleness that God honors and he blesses. Some men (even saved men) do not understand how to treat a woman. So instead of adding fuel to the fire, a Godly wife should walk gently so that her husband may begin to see God in her (this also applies to unsaved husbands). In other words, don't argue him down on his responsibility, rather walk upright, pray, be the example that God has called you to be, and let God deal with him. It is vital to note that it is extremely important to marry a saved man because when you can't reach him...God can! However, if you find yourself married to an unsaved man my recommendation is to take 1 Peter 3:1-7 to heart, to mind, and to action.

#3 The Holy Spirit undergirds us

In other words, the Holy Spirit supports us. If you are a woman and have a little something extra on those thighs, hips, and mid-section you are probably familiar with a God sent product called "Spanx". Can we just stop right here for two seconds to give God the praise for the things that he has done? I mean they are really helping some of us…right?!?! When a wife undergirds her husband, she supports him. Now, here is the God's truth – nobody is perfect, and if you've been married any amount of time and there were a line for unperfect people you and your husband would probably be the first in line. The truth is nobody is perfect. You can't support your husband only when he does what you think is correct. You must support him when you don't agree with him and, as I said earlier, let the Lord deal with him. We are supposed to support and let God do the rest. If you go back to my early example of Abigail and Nabel, you see a woman who pretty much knows who she is dealing with. Her husband is far from perfect, yet she still covers him. David and his men would have wrecked poor Nabel's life, but his wife stood in the gap and did what was necessary to help her husband. You are more like the Holy Spirit when you learn the art of undergirding your husband.

#4 The Holy Spirit guides us to truth

In other words, the Holy Spirit points us to truth, but not only that, the Holy Spirts gives us power to accept the truth. Think about the disciples and their ultimate deaths. I mean ALL but John died absolutely horrible deaths, not for a lie, but for truth. You are to help point your husband toward truth. You don't have to do it through nagging and fighting; you can simply live truth. What truth do I mean? Truth that you love him, truth that you believe in him, the truth that he is one of many blessings that the Lord has given you. Who wouldn't want to love and adore a woman who rests in the truth of who her husband is and the blessing he is to her life? I don't know very many men that would not find the truth of who he is to her extremely appealing and profitable; but not only that truth but the Holy Spirit leads us into truth about who God says you are to be for your husband. Here's what the Holy Spirit says you are to be for your husband:

A. Give him sex consistently (See 1 Corinthians 7:1-40)
B. Do him good and not bad, work hard and be honorable (Proverbs 31:10-31)
C. Respect him (Ephesians 5:33)
D. Submit to him (Colossians 3:18)
E. Be helpful (Genesis 2:18)
F. Be wise (Proverbs 31:26)
G. Have self-control (Titus 2:5)

Okay, I have to admit that is a lot but if I had to sum up that list in one sentence, I would sum it up this way.

**God wants a wife to love her husband
by being kind, loving, supportive, wise,
and helpful.**

Last thing on truth: you have to know truth so when you hear a lie you can reject it (period). If you are watching the housewives of whatever and you see a woman on the show not having self-control, I have to admit it's entertaining, don't go out trying to imitate her. That's not of God. If you see your husband cleaning don't just sit there and continue to watch *Law and Order* (well, watch until the commercial) then get up and help him. If your husband says we are not buying a new car right now, don't pull up a month from then with a new Audi. You get it??? To execute the plan of God for Christian wives you must be willing to do all the above or you should NOT consider getting married. Now, for those women already married and you're not doing well with the list above - just start to take it a little at a time. Explain to your husband you know how important it is to comply with the will of God and you will be working on it. Ask him to be patient with you. A couple more pointers before we close this chapter, don't give yourself any excuses. If you fall short... own it. If you miss the mark... own it. We all fall short, so cut yourself some slack and get your head back in the game. Lastly, if complying with "a man" seems to be a difficult pill to swallow, maybe it would be easier to understand that your compliance first starts with God. God wants you to comply with your husband. So, when you walk in cooperation and compliance with your husband you are walking and complying with God. If that doesn't do the trick for you, then please continue to fast and pray because it is God's will that you be blessed and I don't know any better way to be blessed by God than to walk in obedience with His will and His plan for your life and your marriage.

CHAPTER 2

Deborah the Devoted Leader

Leaders Step Up When Needed

In chapter 5 of Judges, the first thing we see is God selling the Israelites into the hands of King Jabin. As I studied for this section of the book, I kept saying, why would God do that? Why would God sell his people into the hands of somebody who would oppress them? Doesn't God know all? The answer is yes, God knows all. So, if God knows all, why would He allow the Israelites to be sold to an evil and dangerous oppressor like King Jabin? The answer is chastisement. God loved them enough to chastise them to bring about the change necessary for genuine repentance. Could you imagine what would happen if God would have left them alone? Can I make this personal? Could you imagine where you and I'd be if God left us alone when we were in sin? He could have let you and I die in our transgressions, but He didn't. That's why we see God selling them into slavey because He had to get their attention in one way or another. He does the same for us. He loves us so He allows things to happen so we will repent and turn back to Him. I liken it to our own children. When they behave poorly, we put them on a time out, or sentence them to their room for the evening, or whatever it is you do to subdue them. You do it because you know if they continue that type of behavior they are going to have a very difficult life. You get their attention so they understand what they did was wrong. I remember when my youngest child, Marshall, was a little boy. He was a stubborn little guy. I was punishing him for something he did. Marshall crawled under the bed to avoid standing in the corner. I looked under the bed and told him to come out. He refused so I said, "then I guess we'll be here all night long." He said, "I guess we will." Well guess what? We were there all night long because he was stiff-necked and refused to come out. That's the type of people the Israelites were. They were stiff-necked. It took them twenty years of oppression before they finally called out to God for help. But as we know God turns evil into good and He turned it around for the Israelites by sending a new leader to get them out of the mess they found themselves in (again). Deborah comes on the scene as a seasoned leader. She was already judging cases for the Israelites in her own unique way. She wasn't just holding court, but she was doing it under a tree so the people would not be too hot while they waited for her guidance. That's hashtag #sowomanlike she probably had somebody giving out water or lemonade. It is important to note that God will give elevation when you are faithful over your preceding role. You can't jump to pastor without first being a minister. You can't become a deacon without first attending church on a regular basis. We have to be faithful over preceding roles before God can elevate us to new roles (see Matthew 25:23). It is now time for Deborah to lead the fighting men into battle. She tells Barak to take 10,000 men up to Mount Tabor and she would lead Jabin's commander, Sisera, to the Kishon River and give him into his hands and he could take it from there. The first thing to note is that she (as a leader) moves by the Spirit.

"She sent for Barak son of Abinoam from Kedesh in Naphtali and said to him, '**_The Lord, the God of Israel, commands you:_** "Go, take with you ten thousand men of Naphtali and Zebulun and lead them up to Mount Tabor"'" (Judges 4:6, emphasis added).

Please note if you are going to be an effective Christian leader you have to lead with the power of God. Don't ever try to lead something spiritual with your natural abilities. Your natural abilities may work at work or playing sports, but the things of the Spirit have to be led by the Spirit. Devotion to God can never be done naturally because naturally we walk in disobedience and defiance when we don't see the whole picture. Devotion to God can only be done by the Spirit. The Spirit of God will make you say "yes, Lord" when you want to say no. The Spirit of God will make you go when you want to stay. Zechariah 4:6 says it best: "Not by might, nor by power, BUT by my Spirit, says the Lord of host."

Deborah the Confident Leader

In the book of Judges, we see three types of people. We see:
- People who love God
- People who pretend to love God
- People who don't love God

Deborah without question was a person who loved God, and because of her love for God she was courageous because she understood that God has her back. We can walk in confidence when we know that God has us. It doesn't matter what people say or what people do. The fact is…God has you! Judges 1:19 says "The Lord was with Judah, and he took possession of the hill country, but could not drive out the inhabitants of the plain, because they had chariots of iron." We already know they had 900 chariots of iron but that is no match for the people who serve an omnipotent God...right? The answer is "right." The issue is not God, the issue is the Israelites faith in God. It was not uncommon for the Israelites to defeat chariots. They did it in:
- Exodus 14:7-29
- Joshua 11:1-8
- 1 Kings 20:21

The Bible is clear that Christians should have faith in the God that they serve and not look at obstacles that seem impossible as being too big for God.

> *"Some take pride in chariots, and some in horses, but our pride is in the name of the Lord our God" (Psalm 20:7).*

Going back to the chariots in Judges 1:19, the chariots represent strong things that seem impossible. It was the chariots that intimidated the Israelites, so instead of doing what God said, which was to remove the Canaanites from the land, they allowed what they saw to determine what they did. So they decided to let the Canaanites live among them although they knew that God was with them. Now, bring this story to what is happening in many of our lives today. There are some iron chariots, some strong things, some huge obstacles, that need to be removed from our lives that God has given you dominion over but that you will not remove because of fear. You're afraid of how things will work without it. You're afraid of the backlash of removing it. You're afraid that your life is going to have to change if you remove it. You know what God has spoken but you refuse to remove the chariots of iron because of fear. Here's what you need to know – there are consequences for allowing strong things to remain that you have the power to remove. The consequences for the Israelites were not sudden but gradual. Overtime they began to serve the gods of the Canaanites. They began to be influenced by the Canaanites and drifted further and further from the will of God. Anytime we refuse to drive the things of this world completely out of our lives we will drift from the will of God. It's like following somebody in a car. If you don't follow close enough eventually you will lose sight of them or, even if you don't lose complete visibility, you will leave room for others to get in front of you which gives you limited visibility to the car you are supposed to be following. We cannot afford to lose visibility of God. One thing we can clearly identify as a strong leadership trait of Deborah is her ability to stay connected to God even with major obstacles in her way.

Deborah the Courageous Leader

I remember when I was a young woman there was an equally young women, just a bit older than me, in a leadership role. She was pregnant and went to the doctor for a checkup. We expected her to be back by 1pm so when we noticed she had not returned back we began to get a little concerned. Around 3:30 our manager called me into his office and said, "Are you ready?" To which I said, "Ready for what?" and he said, "Ready to fill in for Britney? She's been placed on bed rest." I said, "Of course." The reason I could confidently say that I was ready is because I had already been preparing for that moment. I already learned everything I needed to know about Britney's job. I knew at some point she'd be taking off on leave. I learned how to open the store, close the store, fix issues that typically Britney would handle, etc., in preparation to step up when I was needed. Deborah was not just at the right place at the right time. She was there for such a time as this. Deborah heard God tell her to go get Barak and give him these instructions:

Now Deborah, a prophetess, the wife of Lapidoth, was judging Israel at that time. 5 [i]And she would sit under the palm tree of Deborah between Ramah and Bethel in the mountains of Ephraim. And the children of Israel came up to her for judgment. 6 Then she sent and called for [j]Barak the son of Abinoam from [k]Kedesh in Naphtali, and said to him, "Has not the Lord God of Israel commanded, 'Go and [l]deploy troops at Mount [l]Tabor; take with you ten thousand men of the sons of Naphtali and of the sons of Zebulun; 7 and against you [m]I will deploy Sisera, the commander of Jabin's army, with his chariots and his multitude at the [n]River Kishon; and I will [2]deliver him into your hand'?"

(Judges 4:4-7)

But what seems strange is Barak doesn't want to do it alone. He insists that Deborah go with him (see below).

8 And Barak said to her, "If you will go with me, then I will go; but if you will not go with me, I will not go!"

*9 So she said, "I will surely go with you; nevertheless there will be no glory for you in the journey you are taking, for the Lord will ᵉsell Sisera into the **hand of a woman.**" Then Deborah arose and went with Barak to Kedesh.*

(Judges 4:8-9, emphasis added)

I believe God is all knowing (Omniscient). Which means he knows it all. I do not believe that it took God by surprise that Barak didn't want to step up alone. I believe it was divine design from the start. God didn't need anybody's approval to slide Deborah into the forefront, but for Deborah's sake I believe God offered it to Barak first. Once Barak declined unless Deborah goes with him is when Deborah had the green light to move forward in her destiny. Above you see I've put the words **"hand of a woman"** in bold and underlined it. Deborah was purposeful with that statement. Think about it. If she was a man, she wouldn't need to highlight that the Lord was going to give Sisera into the hand of a man. No, it was almost as if Deborah was saying to Barak "you had your chance to do what is customary BUT I'm not going to convince you to take your rightful place. God is speaking and somebody is going to move. Either you or me! Oh, you don't want to move? Then I'll move and let me spell out what that means. God is going to get the victory using me, a woman (yes, a woman), to set the Israelites free." Here's the point, my sister in Christ, God may be calling you. It is up to you to answer the call with no apologies. Anybody who cannot accept it, let it be their problem, not yours. Answer the call then walk in the call.

Deborah the Bee

Deborah's name means bee. She can be sweet yet strong. When I think of a bee, I think of a little bug that can hurt me yet a little bug that produces a wonderful product. Bees are very interesting and valuable creatures. Did you know that for every 3 pieces of food you ingest the bee's footprint is somewhere in it. Maurice Maeterlinck says that the bee is so important to the world that if they failed to exist the human race would as well[2] (sounds like a woman, huh?). Another interesting fact about bees is they are extremely structured and purpose driven. It is how they were designed. The pollination they provide for our crops is crucial for the world. The bee itself is unclean but what they provide (honey) is clean. Isn't that just like God? How He can create something that is unclean and make it produce something clean. The testimony of every Christian should be that of a bee. We, "the unclean," are to proclaim the clean, holy, and matchless name of Jesus. This is why I have a hard time buying into the "I don't go to church because they are all hypocrite's theory." We are unclean! We are all hypocrites! We the imperfect are called to preach, teach, and declare the perfect gospel of Jesus Christ. Of course we are hypocrites. I believe there is an unfair pressure put on Christians to be perfect and when it is discovered that we are not, the tendency is to take it out on God. The problem with this concept is it blames the perfect for the sins of the unperfect and places the accuser in direct conflict with the will of God which is an extremely dangerous place to be. The people of God must understand this and therefore do everything we can to exemplify the goodness of God; however, people must understand that the Christian is not perfect so when we do wrong, they should count it to us and not God. That's another book for another day, but the point is bees are a great example for the structure of salvation.

We are sinful but God took our sins and poured them upon Him (Jesus) and produced the sweet grace of salvation.

CHAPTER 3

Deborah the Beautiful

As I read Judges 4 and 5, I see that Deborah is brave, smart, loyal, obedient, and wise. What I don't see is any mention of her appearance. Were Deborah's looks not worth mentioning? We do see the Bible seemingly mentioning beauty when it describes certain women of the Bible such as:

- Rachel
- Sarai
- Esther
- Vashti
- Bathsheba

All these women were physically beautiful and served a purpose beyond their looks great enough to be written in the Bible, however we don't see Deborah's outward beauty ever being noted. I want to start this chapter looking at all the women above and how beauty did not solve any of their problems nor did it matter at all outside of being mentioned as mere words.

Rachel

*[17] Leah had weak[a] eyes, **but Rachel had a lovely figure and was beautiful.** [18] Jacob was in love with Rachel and said, 'I'll work for you seven years in return for your younger daughter Rachel'"* (Genesis 29:17-18, emphasis added).

The story of Rachel is that of a love tringle between Rachel, her husband Jacob, and her sister Leah. The back story is Jacob loved Rachel so much that he was willing to work for his Uncle

Laban for seven years to obtain her. On their wedding night, to his surprise, it was not his blushing bride Rachel but her older sister Leah. Jacob goes back to his uncle Laban for clarification to which his uncle explained that it was not customary for the youngest daughter to wed first so he'd have to take Leah (since she was the oldest) and then he could have Rachel. Did I mention he had to work an additional seven years for Rachel because the first seven years was for Leah? That's right, Jacob worked seven years for someone he did not want but was so committed to the women that he did want that he worked an additional seven years just so he could marry her. Now that's love! The story goes on that Leah had no problem giving Jacob children, but Rachel was barren and could not conceive a child with Jacob. It was frustrating to Rachel to see her husband having children with Leah and she not being able to, so she told her husband that he needed to give her children or she would die (Genesis 30:1). But the Lord did not see fit to give her a child at that time. Fast forward many years and add 2 other women to the picture who bore children by Jacob and what you have is a complete mess. Ultimately, God did eventually allow Rachel to have a child named Joseph. It was Rachel's beauty that attracted Jacob to her. Ultimately, it worked together for the good because Rachel bore Joseph who was a type and shadow of Jesus Christ, but the point remains that character trumps beauty every time. The lesson that we learn from this story is beauty will fade! It's just a matter of time; however, the internal depth that a person obtains through years of facing and fighting trials is what's most important. We also learn that unchecked jealousy will block your blessings. Both sisters had some level of jealousy for one another. Jealousy will blind you to what is right in the Lord's sight and have you in a place of discord and discomfort, robbing you of a healthy, peaceful life that God wants you to have. Lastly, we learn that we don't always get what we want but God still expects faith out of us. Leah wanted to be desired and loved by her husband, however she was not. Rachel wanted children and initially she was not able to conceive but God still expects faithfulness from His people even in difficult situations. There is nothing wrong with beauty, but it is no match for being a woman of faith, substance, and spirituality. Like we take care of our nails, hair, make-up, and all the things we believe make us beautiful, we should spend just as much time in the things of God because the things of God will take us into eternity and everything else (in time) will fade.

> *Do not love the world or anything in the world.*
> *If anyone loves the world, love for the Father is*
> *not in them.* ¹⁶ *For everything in the world—the*
> *lust of the flesh, the lust of the eyes, and the pride*
> *of life—comes not from the Father but from the*
> *world. The world and its desires pass away, but*
> *whoever does the will of God lives forever.*
>
> 1 John 2:15-17

Esther

"*He was bringing up Hadassah, that is Esther, the daughter of his uncle, for she had neither father nor mother. The young woman had* ***a beautiful figure and was lovely to look at,*** *and when her father and her mother died, Mordecai took her as his own daughter*" (Esther 2:7, emphasis added).

The story of Esther is a story of a women who was attractive, brave, and spiritual. I note this because she had a beautiful body and a beautiful face, but in addition to that she had substance. As I studied for this chapter of the book, I didn't want women to walk away thinking they needed to throw away their lip gloss and spanks, but rather understand that being outwardly beautiful is not an issue for God nor should it be for them. God is okay with you being beautiful, however God wants more than beauty out of us. God wants us to still honor him and be brave, smart, and courageous women of faith. Esther is a beautiful woman, but she is also spiritual and brave. Esther was raised by Mordecai (her cousin) after both her parents died. She became a queen after the king divorced his wife (Queen Vashti). She was a Jew, but she was advised to conceal that information by her cousin Mordecai. Esther, with other women, was taken to a citadel so they could strut their stuff before the king, sort of like they were in a beauty pageant. Esther quickly became the front runner to the king's heart. Eventually, Esther was chosen to be the next queen. She won even greater favor with the king after her cousin Mordecai overheard a plot to assassinate the king. Keep in mind that Esther was a Jew and so was her cousin Mordecai. Jews would not bow to anybody but God. When Mordecai was asked to bow to Haman he refused. The ramifications of Mordecai's stance to not bow to Haman was to kill all Jews. Upon hearing this Mordecai pleaded with the queen to do something about it, but she feared for her own life. Eventually, Esther did step in and called for a three day fast. After the fast, Queen Esther approached her husband, the king, and asked that he attend a banquet set for the next day. That night the king could not sleep so he decided to read a book about his reign as king. In the book the king was reminded of the plot to assassinate him and that plot being exposed by Mordecai. This next day at the banquet the king asked Queen Esther what she wanted. It was then that Esther asked that her people not be killed and revealed to the king Haman's plan to kill all the Jews for money. Haman was hanged for his deception and was hanged on the same pole he planned to hang Mordecai. The Jews were saved by the bravery and spirituality of Queen Esther. Here's the point...God made some women outwardly beautiful and there is nothing wrong with that, however his plan was never designed for beauty to be the only thing a woman could offer to this world. I think it's interesting that Queen Esther didn't seem to downplay her looks or pretend that she wasn't beautiful. She was more than a pretty face, but she used her pretty face to position herself for a better life and ultimately God used her position that she obtained through her beauty to save his people. Notice that we see Esther's beauty being noted at the beginning of her story, but that theme seems to simmer down, and her true, inner greatness seems to take front street. There is nothing wrong with beauty. Use it! Not to take advantage or manipulate, but use it for God's glory. You're more than a face and a body. You were created for greatness so use what you got to advance the kingdom and save those you can in the process. There is somebody around you that needs you to step out of the bubble of cuteness into greatness. They are depending on you. They are waiting on you. Be cute and courageous, but do it for the glory of God.

> *"For if you keep silent at this time, relief and deliverance will rise for the Jews from another place, but you and your father's house will perish. And who knows whether you have not come to the kingdom for such a time as this?"*
>
> *Esther 4:14*

Sarai
"As he was about to enter Egypt, he said to his wife Sarai, 'I know what a beautiful woman you are'" (Genesis 12:11).

Sarai was another woman noted as beautiful in the Bible. In the book of Genesis her husband pauses and notes her beauty. But again, outward beauty does not void us of problems. In the story of Sarai, or Sarah, we see a woman barren. She wants children and pretty much has given up on the idea of having one. So she decides to give her maidservant Hagar to her husband to produce a child. Just like in the story of Rachel, she has taken action into her own hands. The story goes on that Rachel ended up having a mess of a situation on her hands because her and Hagar are at war with one another. Eventually Hagar and her son, Ishmael, were banished to the desert because of the tension between the two. Once Sarah had her son Isaac there was no need for Hagar, so she was thrown away like a person would throw away trash. Here's the point Sarah was noted as beautiful but again beauty did not solve any of her problems nor did it make any difference in her life. Hating someone because they are just as beautiful as you does not accomplish God's righteousness. Taking it a step further, using someone then throwing them away after you no longer need them does not accomplish God's righteousness either. Beauty is a great thing but, as noted previously in this chapter, it will eventually fade for us all to some degree or another. Just as we are searching for that magic serum or the new and improved skin care routine to slow down the aging process, we should also be looking for ways in which we can reflect the God that is in us. Don't let jealousy or envy distract you from the race. Believe me, there's enough beauty to go around. We can all be beautiful in our own rights but more than anything beauty truly comes from within. I have seen some drop-dead gorgeous women until they begin to speak. Once they speak words that are vulgar and ungodlily, they don't seem as attractive anymore. Why? Because what is on the inside will eventually come to the outside. If you're a mess on the inside, it's just a matter of time before somebody will see it on the outside. Outward beauty means nothing when compared to inward beauty that is stored up in a woman's heart from a place of discipline and obedience to the God she serves.

> *[18] But what comes out of the mouth proceeds from the heart, and this defiles a person. [19] For out of the heart come evil thoughts, murder, adultery, sexual immorality, theft, false witness, slander. [20] These are what defile a person.*
>
> *Matthew 15:18-20(a)*

Queen Vashti

"In the seventh day, when King Xerxes was in high spirits from wine, he commanded the seven eunuchs who served him—Mehuman, Biztha, Harbona, Bigtha, Abagtha, Zethar and Karkas— ¹¹ to bring before him Queen Vashti, wearing her royal crown, **in order to display her beauty to the people and nobles, for she was lovely to look at"** *(Esther 1:10-11, emphasis added).*

Often when I hear this story, I hear people holding Queen Vashti up as a Godly women who was under a drunkard and foolish husband. Typically, this narrative is painted because the king asked her to walk naked in front the entire citadel of Susa wearing only her crown, to which she refused. I agree with why it seemed like a ridiculous request; however, not only was he her husband, but he was the king. Honestly, I would have had a hard time complying with such a request as well, but Vashti was wrong way before this request was ever uttered. In chapter 1 the king throws a party first for the nobles spanning from Persia to Media, then he throws a second party for the least to the greatest in his kingdom. The rich, the poor, the everybody in-between, but Queen Vashti threw her own party on the same day but with only the elitist women. Her husband, the king, threw a party for everybody, but she decided to do her own thing with the best women of the region. Did she think she was too good to hang out with the commoners? Did she think she was too good to hang out with her drunk husband, no matter what his status was? Was she better than the women at the party her husband was throwing? We don't know, but what we do know is she had to be summoned to the king's party. Was the king making an example of her since she shamed him by not being an active participant in his party? Was this the king's way of demonstrating to her and the rest of the region that he had control over his wife? Again, these are questions that we do not know the answer to, but what we do know is Vashti knew her husband. Clearly, he was prone to overindulge in wine. Clearly he was the king and clearly he was throwing a party for everybody, the choice and the commoner alike. Wives are to be help meets to their husbands and it does not appear that she was doing that. We don't know if she thought she was too cute to join the party or if she didn't want to be bothered with her husband because he was behaving in a way that was unbecoming of a king, but what we do know is she was not supporting or walking in obedience as a wife. So while the request was wrong and embarrassing, the root of it could be her husband feeling disrespected and therefore acting out to possibly send a message to the kingdom. Here's the point... our looks nor money make us better than anyone else. We must be very careful as women to not get so hung up in the exterior that we forget that God expects obedience no matter what you look like or who you are. Vashti wasn't just disobedient to her husband, but she was also disrespectful to God who placed her as a help meet to the king, her husband. God expects obedience for all his people. He, unlike man, will settle for nothing less.

> *16 Don't you know that when you offer yourselves to someone as obedient slaves, you are slaves of the one you obey—whether you are slaves to sin, which leads to death, or to obedience, which leads to righteousness?*
>
> *Romans 6:16*

Bathsheba

"One evening David got up from his bed and walked around on the roof of the palace. From the roof he saw a woman bathing. The woman was very beautiful" (2 Samuel 11:2).

The story of Bathsheba is a story of a woman whose beauty captivated the king to the point and place where he had to call for her. This call to the king ended with Bathsheba pregnant with a child. By all accounts, you'd think this was great news. Bathsheba is now pregnant with the king's baby. The problem is that Bathsheba was married. Yikes! She was married to a man named Uriah. Once David found out that she was pregnant he tried to conceal it and when that did not work, he got Uriah killed. The story goes on that David and Bathsheba's baby died which left both severely depressed. Ultimately, they both moved on and had a son named Solomon. Bathsheba is often painted as a bad girl of the Bible. I disagree because I'm not sure what she could have done. I don't think not going when summoned by the king is the correct response and I don't think you say no when the king wants to sleep with you (at least in that time period). I think David misused his power and put her in a no-win situation. What I love about Bathsheba was her ability to be able to move forward. She mourned but she moved forward and was the vessel to birth King Solomon into the world. Here's the point, beautiful women typically get attention and sometimes it's the wrong attention. Although the attention that Bathsheba got was not her fault, she preserved her life by complying with such a powerful man. She experienced the loss of a baby and the deep pain that type of experience can cause. The loss of a child has to be one of the most painful experiences a mother can experience. Maybe you haven't experienced the loss of a child, but you've experienced the loss of a dream, or a marriage, or maybe even a parent. Loss of any kind can be a painful experience but try to be like Bathsheba and fight through it. The reason we fight through it is because God will impregnate us again. He will allow us to dream again, but He can't do that unless we still have some fight left in us. He can't do that unless we trust and believe that He has plans for us and His plan is to help us and not harm us (Jeremiah 29:11). Beauty does not omit pain, in fact sometimes beauty is the cause of pain. Bathsheba is the perfect example of beauty getting her into a huge mess to begin with. Most of the other women noted earlier in this chapter to some degree, or another caused the pain that they were in. I don't see that in the life of Bathsheba. She seems to be the innocent victim, yet she persevered and her name is forever attached to two great men of faith, King David and King Solomon.

> *20 Now to him who is able to do immeasurably more than all we ask or imagine, according to his power that is at work within us, 21 to him be glory in the church and in Christ Jesus throughout all generations, for ever and ever! Amen.*
>
> *Ephesians 3:20-21*

CHAPTER 4

Deborah the Woke

'Wake up, wake up, Deborah!
  Wake up, wake up, break out in song!
Arise, Barak!
  Take captive your captives, son of Abinoam.'

Judges 5:12

I remember being in a conversation with a person about how "woke" they were. Woke, for those who may not know is a term being used to express a person's awakening, so to speak. It's a term used to express that they now know something they did not know before. We were talking about the need to attend church in a modern-day society. My thoughts were that of course church is vitally important to all believers, and he felt that it was unnecessary in the world of today. He kept reminding me throughout the conversation that he was "woke." Finally, he got so frustrated with me that he told me that I was not woke. Now, of course I'd rather stay asleep if it means turning my back on what is clearly the will of God for all Christians, which is to attend church regularly, but the point is he felt that I was asleep for not keeping up with the times. That conversation is what has inspired this chapter of the book. Deborah was told by God to "Wake up." I don't know if she was off base in some way or if she was losing momentum, but I do see God telling her to wake up because it was time to move His people to a new level and a new dimension. I believe we all have moments in our Christian walk where we hear God pressing upon our hearts to wake up. For some of us, He's telling us to wake up because we are sinning against Him. For some, it is to wake up because something is happening in our families, and we need to pay close attention. For some of us it could be to wake up to a whole new dimension of anointing. I did think it was interesting that He told Deborah to wake up but told Barak to arise. Deborah was in wait mode. She waited while her nation worshipped idols. She waited while her nation was strong armed and oppressed by the Canaanites. What I love about Deborah was although she waited, she did not waiver. You don't see her losing faith or falling apart, you see she is solid, still, and unmovable in the work to which she was called.

> **"4 Now Deborah, a prophet, the wife of Lappidoth, was leading[a] Israel at that time. 5 She held court under the Palm of Deborah between Ramah and Bethel in the hill country of Ephraim, and the Israelites went up to her to have their disputes decided"**
> **(Judges 4:4-6).**

This is what spiritual leaders do until they are called. They don't wait for their time to shine and then take center stage they wait and work and move as they are told by the Holy Spirit. We see that in the story of David (1 Samuel 16:1-12). David, who was tending sheep, was doing the work that was assigned to him and Samuel called for him after rejecting his brothers. It was there that God anointed him to be king but until that happened, he was working. We also see it in the story of Ruth (Ruth 3-5). Ruth is working when she is noticed by Boaz and by chapter 5 she marries him. She didn't stop working for any purpose other than to rest. God wants us to wait on Him and work until it's time for our next level.

Deborah the Proclaimer

Once you are "woke" the expectation is to proclaim this new-found "wokeness" (not a word but you get it). A good spiritual leader will always raise up other leaders because they understand it is a kingdom principle. Where would Timothy be without a Paul? Where would Esther be without Mordecai? Where would Elisha be without Elijah? Good leaders will always raise someone else up to greatness. The Bible supports teamwork. See scriptures below:

- **Nehemiah 4:** When the Israelites were rebuilding the wall in Jerusalem, the work got tough, and they got discouraged. Finally, they just gave up. So, Nehemiah reorganized the work into teams. Half would stand guard with their spears and swords and protect everyone. The other half would work. Then they'd alternate their positions. He posted everyone by groups and families, so they could encourage and support each other.

- **Ecclesiastes 4:9-12:** "Two are better off than one, because together they can work more effectively. If one of them falls down, the other can help him up. But if someone is alone and falls, it's just too bad, because there is no one to help him. If it's cold, two can sleep together and stay warm but how can you keep warm by yourself. Two men can resist an attack that would defeat one man alone. A rope of three cords is hard to break" (GNT). We are better together than we are on our own.

- **Acts 24:** Paul specifically mentions seven people who were part of his ministry team. He brought others along, not only to train them, but also to keep him encouraged.

- **Mark 6:7:** When Jesus sent people out in ministry He sent them out in twos. He did not expect them to minister alone.

Deborah understood that her role was to wake up and give instruction as the prophetess of God but it was Barak's job to go and fight. She proclaimed the word and instruction from God to Barak so that the work of the Lord would continue. When Nehemiah was building the wall there were distractions, complications, setbacks, and set ups yet he continued to work no matter what. He was even tempted to come and get involved in a situation with men that were stirring up mess. They didn't come to him once but three times, doing everything they could to stop his progress, but he refused to come down from the wall. He told the men that he was doing a great work and could not come down from doing the work of the Lord to talk with them. That's what good leaders do when they are working for the Lord. They keep on going and continue to build. They give instruction to other leaders and hold them accountable for their share of the work. They allow other people to be great. They push people to their next level and refuse to allow them to take the easy route out. That's what we see with Deborah. She is pushing Barak toward his part of the work, understanding that God has gifted him for that portion of the work. She first waited, then she woke up, and then she proclaimed the word of the Lord to Barak so he could continue with his portion of the work. My question to you as you read this is: Are you spiritually woke? What are you proclaiming in someone else's life? Many of us spend a great deal of time building ourselves through self-help books, classes etc., but not enough time building others up. Think about how great the Kingdom of God would be if we would start building not for our own advancement but the advancement of the Kingdom through our pouring of knowledge and insight into someone else that they might take hold of their own call that the Kingdom will continue to grow and flourish. That's what God wants from His people and that's what we should be doing for the sake of God and His kingdom. Christ builds!

Deborah the unstoppable

"⁸ Barak said to her, 'If you go with me, I will go; but if you don't go with me, I won't go.'

⁹ 'Certainly I will go with you,'" said Deborah. 'But because of the course you are taking, the honor will not be yours, for the Lord will deliver Sisera into the hands of a woman.' So Deborah went with Barak to Kedesh" (Judges 4:8-9).

God told Deborah to wake up and told Deborah to tell Barak to rise up, but Barak did not want to do it unless Deborah went with him. This is significant because this shows his faith was not in God but in Deborah. Honestly, I don't want to be too hard on Barak because many of us put our faith in everybody but God. We put our faith in a spouse or faith in a job. When tough times come we are very likely to talk to everybody else before God. Deborah was unstoppable because when Barak gave her the ultimatum to go only if she went, that is when prophetically she told him that she would go but the credit would not go to him but to a women. Later in the book you will see why I say she spoke prophetically. Deborah was unstoppable and brave, speaking to a man and telling him what the Lord had spoken to him, addressing his fear head on and matter of fact, telling him exactly what the consequences of his lack of faith would be. I think this would be a great time to address if a women can have spiritual authority over a man. The answer just using this text is absolutely. Deborah was a female. Deborah spoke prophetically to him. Deborah told him what God told her (sounds like a preacher, correct?). When he rejected the request, Deborah told him the consequences without blinking an eye. The last time I checked, when someone tells someone else the consequence of a behavior they are operating from a place of authority. This last point is not to start a debate, but it is to say that God has called some women to walk in the spirit of Deborah and, by the way,

I don't think the spirit of Deborah is exclusive to an unmarried women. I believe a married woman can operate in this spirit, just not over her own husband. Remember Deborah was married but we don't see any indication of her interacting with her husband in that way. When I think of powerful married women of God who I believe operate with a Deborah anointing I think of women like:

Joyce Meyer
Sarah Jakes
Cindy Trim
Victoria Osteen
Medina Pullings
Beth Moore

These are all women I greatly respect for the anointing they have on their life as well as the submissiveness and honor they give to their husbands. Deborah was unstoppable because she walked in obedience by first hearing the voice of God telling her to wake up, which she did. She is unstoppable because she allowed another person to walk in their call. She is unstoppable because when he would not go without her she pivoted so the will of God could be accomplished. Lastly, she is unstoppable because she walked in the prophetic by telling Barak who would get the credit for this victory. Deborah was unstoppable.

CHAPTER 5

Deborah and Lappidoth

Part of this chapter will be dedicated to Lappidoth the husband of Deborah. We don't know much about him other than he was the husband of Deborah. That's pretty much it! He is mentioned in the Bible not because of himself but because of his wife, Deborah. Who we marry is critically important to our success, especially in the spiritual realm. I certainly thank God for every husband that allows his wife to be great, not because she brings home a hefty check or because she was great before she met him so by default, he has to accept it. No, I'm grateful to the men of God who will allow their wives to be great because he recognizes greatness is in her. I believe a husband has many duties as the head of the house. This is the design God has set up. God gives a man authority and responsibility over his wife. I think far too many men focus on the authority and leave out the responsibility. Below you will see some (just some) examples of how Christ loved the church and, since husbands are called to love their wives as Christ loved the church, he now is responsible to execute in the life of his family and specifically his wife (Ephesians 5:25).

First, Christ does not condemn the church, although he could. He does not point out the weaknesses of the church, although he could. He does not beat his chest and demand submissiveness from the church. He loves the church.

Here's how Christ loves the church and how husbands are supposed to love their wives. Again, it's not just authority it is responsibility.

Christ stands with the church.

"And I tell you that you are Peter, and on this rock, I will build my church, and the gates of Hades will not overcome it" Matthew 16:18.

When Peter declared who Jesus was, once asked directly by Jesus, it was there that Jesus tells him in essence "you nailed it, you are absolutely right." Peter knew who Christ was and for that Jesus makes a bold statement to Peter and to all believers, which is, "I will forever stand with the church." Nothing will make me depart from her. It was a declaration after Peter first acknowledged the truth of who Christ was. A husband has authority over his wife as Christ has authority over the church, but he also has responsibility to now stand with his wife as Christ stands with the church and declares nothing, not even hell, will overcome it. Christ loves the church and He stands by the church as a husband should love his wife and stand by his wife. Let me be clear, the church has a lot that it needs to improve on, however Christ is still standing with us through it all. Flaws and all Christ continues to be faithful to a very flawed church. And so, a husband should stand with his wife even with her flaws and love her, correct her, and guide her toward better.

He is an example of faithfulness

"28 Keep watch over yourselves and all the flock of which the Holy Spirit has made you overseers. Be shepherds of the church of God,[a] which he bought with his own blood" (Acts 20:28).

This portion of Acts is Paul giving a farewell speech. Paul's speech has three components.

1. His past ministry
2. His present ministry

3. His future ministry

He encourages the people to stay faithful as he's been faithful for the past three years of ministry in that region. He reminds them that it has been very difficult because of the opposition he's faced. He tells them in essence his faithfulness has not just been to show up but to be faithful to the study and execution of the gospel by way of his teaching ministry. This is important to note because if a husband is to love his wife as Christ loved the church, he must understand the example of faithfulness he must show to his wife not just future forward but in a past tense. Many Christian women want to be sure their husbands are faithful in the marriage, but we should also be concerned that he be an example of faithfulness to God in the past, present, and future tense. Paul is an example of faithfulness to the Lord no matter what was going on in his life and God chose him for that reason. He knew that Paul would be faithful. Paul understood the level of commitment he needed to be an effective ambassador of Christ, and so a husband has to understand that same level of faithfulness is needed to be effective in the kingdom as well as in his marriage. Men are one example to their wives of the faithfulness of God.

He gives good counsel to the church

"*16 Let the message of Christ dwell among you richly as you teach and admonish one another with all wisdom through psalms, hymns, and songs from the Spirit, singing to God with gratitude in your hearts" (Colossians 3:16).*

In this scripture Paul is saying let go of the old thought process and let the new message of Christ take full control over every part of your life. He wants Christians to share it with the world as well as share it with one another THROUGH psalms and hymns in their hearts to God with gratitude and appreciation on their lips. How does this tie into a man's responsibility over his wife? It's the husband taking the lead by living this out by way of example to his wife in real time with other Christians. One struggle that I've seen while serving as a relationship coach is husbands many times are not able to spiritually lead their wives because wives are leading or leaving their husbands spiritually. What do I mean? Many times (not always) wives are the examples of Christian living and not husbands. It's the wives that lead the family to church while the husband follows suit. It's the wives keeping the children and herself involved in a local church not the husbands. It's the wife encouraging her husband to get involved at the church. She leads grace at the dinner table, she inserts Christ in the daily walk of her family. When I say leaves her husband, I mean she will spiritually leave him behind. If he does not follow suit, she will go on without him and get involved in church and then get her children involved. If he chooses not to participate, she simply moves on without him spiritually. I remember having a conversation with a potential mate and he felt the reason men are not leading, and women are leading in many spiritual places (home, church, relationships), is because women will not step out of the way and allow men to lead. The problem with that theory is a women would not have to step aside and allow a man to lead if men had stayed in place as God designed it. I've noticed on many social media platforms where women seem to be giving instructions on how to "catch a man," or "how to pray for the right man," or "how to know if a man is for you or not," or my favorite "red flags all women should look for while dating." There seems to be a lot of teaching on what women should do to get a man but not as much attention on men learning to be men or, more specifically, Christian men. So women are left with the desire to be married and to wait and pray for their Boaz and ultimately Nabal shows up disguised as Boaz. It gets worse... she doesn't realize he's Nabal until she's already in love or in desperation (catch me in the spirit on that one), so she ends up wasting a lot of time crying over his Nabel like activities or personality traits that she misses Boaz altogether. For those who are reading this, and you can see yourself in what I just wrote, please understand if you are not married to Nabel you have no business being Abigail! You have a Deborah spirit that is either active or dormant which means you have 3 choices:

#1 Walk in the Deborah spirit that is already in you

#2 Wake up the Deborah spirit that is dormant in you

#3 Do nothing and, well, do nothing

Ultimately, the choice is yours, but be cautious that nothing from nothing will always lead to nothing (in my Billy Preston voice).

CHAPTER 6

Deborah the Chain Breaker

[13]Then they cried to the Lord in their trouble,
and he saved them from their distress.
[14] He brought them out of darkness,
the utter darkness,
and broke away their chains.
[15] Let them give thanks to the Lord for his
unfailing love and his wonderful deeds
for mankind,
[16] for he breaks down gates of bronze
and cuts through bars of iron.

Psalm 107:13-16

In this chapter I want to explore a chain breaker. By the way, I want to dedicate this section of the book to my spiritual parents, Virgil and Vieta Foster; they truly are prayer warriors, typically behind the scenes pushing ministries forward. They are true examples of pressing for God through extreme obstacles and circumstances. Chain breakers are people who are completely dedicated to prayer as a way of life and I believe because of that they are able to get God's attention when they pray. This is not to say that Christian's who pray on a normal and even consistent regiment can't reach God's spiritual ear, but it is to say that I believe certain people really do pray with genuine faith in what they are praying for. They are chain breakers who are able to reach heaven through words prayed out in faith. There are many prayer warriors in the Bible, but I'd like to highlight three for this chapter:

- Hannah
- Daniel
- David

Hannah (Read 1 Sam 1:1-19)

Hannah was in a mess of a situation. She could not have children, but her husband's other wife could. You know how this story goes because it's happened before in other stories of the Bible. Ultimately, Peninnah (the other wife) taunts Hannah because Hannah can't have children and Hannah is so upset that she cries and prays to God that He will give her a child. Her and her husband (Elkanah) conceive a child and name him Samuel, who turns out to become the last judge in Israel and one of the prophets after the death of Moses. What we learn from Hannah is that prayer works BUT there are some things that she did to position herself so that God could hear her.

#1 Hannah cried out to God THROUGH prayer. God can handle our frustration and our drama. He can handle you and I being frustrated with Him to the point we cry, weep, and yell. He's not going to take it personally. He understands that we don't know what He knows and therefore get frustrated with Him.

#2 Hannah prays like a soldier. She shows up, she is aggressively asking for direction. She is not somber or passive. When a soldier shows up for battle, he/she understands it's no time for games, only action. She is not messing around with her petition of God, she is aggressive and intentional with her ask of God.

#3 She remembers Gods faithfulness. Hannah could pray to God because, clearly, she understood his faithfulness. She knew that having a child was out of her control, but God was still in control and God was faithful.

Daniel (Read Daniel 6)

Daniel was unapologetically for God. When his foes, or as they say nowadays "haters," rose up against him because he had the favor of the king, he remained steadfast and unmovable in his commitment, not to the king so much as the King of Kings. Daniel had done nothing wrong other than following God but yet he ended up in a life-threatening position. He chooses to pray to God even when a decree was given by the king. Disobedience to the decree would not end well for anybody who dared to not obey it but we see Daniel not missing a beat. He heard about the decree and we see the only action he took was to obey God and continue praying. What we see from Daniel is a trust in God that even when facing uncertainty, he understands and holds the position that God is still in control. I want to highlight some additional nuggets God shows us through the tribulation of Daniel.

#1 Do everything you can to keep clean hands. There was nothing his haters could do with him because Daniel was a man of integrity. He walked upright before God. When his haters could not expose his weakness, they laid a trap for him to fall into. They knew he was way too committed to God to stop praying to God so they set a trap that they knew he could not follow.

#2 Never give up on God. Daniel did not stop praying to God although he was perfectly aware of the consequences of not following the decree. Because he was disobedient to the king's decree he was going to be thrown in the lion's den. At no point do we see Daniel giving up on God. We see him continuing to be faithful to God no matter what the situation looks like.

#3 Faithfulness to God will draw people to God. Believe it or not people are watching your walk and it's your walk that can draw or drive people to God. In Daniel's case his faithfulness to God drew in the king and the king decreed that everybody would follow the God of Daniel.

#4 Integrity means nothing if it has never been tested. It's one thing to follow God in words or even in action as long as the action doesn't get you killed. Daniel had the right talk and even walk. He did what God said to do, he prayed three times a day and even when faced with death his obedience to God withstood the test.

It is very easy to follow God when it benefits us, but following God to the point of losing our lives is a completely different commitment level. I truly believe that Daniel's prayer life was an integrate part of his commitment to God even if it meant his life. Daniel is an amazing story of a man who put his very life on the line and refused to pray to anybody other than the God of heaven and of earth. #wow

David (Read Psalm 25:4)

We definitely see David as a prayer warrior. We see throughout the pages of the Old Testament different prayers uttered by David. We see David praying for sin and the result of sin, which is guilt. We see him praying for mercy and deliverance from his enemies, but the one I'd like to focus on in this section of the book is David's prayer for guidance found in Psalm 25. David is asking God for guidance and it doesn't seem his prayer is for any specific reason other than to know what pleases God. I often think Christians pray that God will tell them what to do in one way or another but that doesn't seem to be what David is asking for. It seems David just wants to please God so he's asking for direction on how to do that. His prayer is simple. He says, in essence, show me what you want and teach me how to do it. This is just a side note, but doesn't it seem that some of the best prayers in the Bible are the simplest prayers? David just wants to know the will of God not just for his life but the will of God in life. I thought about my three children who are now adults. I've sacrificed for them and loved them dearly. I've shown them the right way to go and now it's time for them to execute the things I've shown them (at least in my mind). It would be so awesome if one of them would call me and simply said "Mom, what do you want from me?" Not, can you help me with this or that or can you tell me how to cook this or that, but simply, "Mom what would please you today?" I'd probably hit the floor. God wants us to want what He wants. He wants us to be like Jesus when He knew the hour was coming to be crucified. He asked God to take the cup from Him but then quickly remember that it's not His will, but God's will. A chain breaker understands that it's not their will but it's God's will that is the priority. Chain breakers understand they are just the mouthpiece of God. They will pray with specifics but ultimately, they just want the will of the Father to be done but in order to know the will of the Father...you have to want to know Him and do what He wants.

Now that we know some of the stories of chain breakers, let me tell you the three characteristics of a chain breaker.

1. A Chain breaker calls out impurity:
"For he was saying to him, "Come out of the man, you unclean spirit!" (Mark 5:8).

Because a chain breaker has the heart of Christ. He/she understands the importance of calling out an impure spirit. Let me give you a word of caution, which is to clean in front of your own front door first. This is just integrous. You can't call out impure spirits that you've overcome and not call out the impure spirits that you have not. So before you go all John the Baptist on people, be sure you got the plank out of your own eye. When we think of Deborah, we see a brave woman who knew how to call out a few things. She called Barak out on being a coward. She's like, really Barak? We about to do this right now? You're going to wait for me to do what God is calling you to do? Really?!?!

2. A Chain Breaker shines a light in dark places

"6 Now when Herod was about to bring him out, on that very night, Peter was sleeping between two soldiers, bound with two chains, and sentries before the door were guarding the prison. 7 And behold, an angel of the Lord stood next to him, and a light shone in the cell. He struck Peter on the side and woke him, saying, 'Get up quickly.' And the chains fell off his hands" (<u>Acts 12:6-7</u>).

This point is not what you think. It's not that chain breakers point out impurity (only) but they shine light in dark places so that people can wake up THEN get up. There is a difference between waking up and getting up. In the mornings we wake up but we don't always get up on time. Do you know how many times I've been late for something because I woke up but didn't get up on time? Let's just say way too many times. Here's the point, I've spiritually needed to get up when I woke up and it was the chain breakers in my life that shed the light in the dark place to help me find my way out. To the chain breakers that are reading this chapter, you have an obligation which is to shine the light on people who need Christ. You are the flashlight that takes them from darkness and despair and guides them to Christ using the light of the Holy Spirit. What an absolutely amazing opportunity and call that's been placed on your shoulders.

3. A Chain Breaker praises God in all circumstances

"25 About midnight Paul and Silas were praying and singing hymns to God, and the prisoners were listening to them, 26 and suddenly there was a great earthquake, so that the foundations of the prison were shaken. And immediately all the doors were opened, and everyone's bonds were unfastened" (<u>Acts 16:25-26</u>).

I absolutely love this story in the Bible because it's the clear example of how we can't just praise God when times are good. We have to praise God in season and out of season. Paul and Silas were in prison singing and praying and the prisoners heard them.

The prisoners didn't join them, they heard them. Paul and Silas were in the exact same situation as the other's yet they chose to praise and pray to God as their way through. We do have a choice when we are in the prisons of life and that is to praise and pray or to not. Deborah said to Barak we are moving forward, and he chose to let fear rise up instead of faith. He made a choice, and we make choices as well. Do we serve God while in the prisons of life or do we focus on the fact that we are in prison? God is a freewill God. We can choose him, or we can not. Chain breakers understand although there is a choice it's really not a choice. They understand like Peter understood when many turned their backs on Jesus and Jesus asked the twelve "you do not want to leave too?" and Peter said, "to whom shall we go." Chain breakers understand there is really one way and that is the way of the Lord. And I for one am eternally grateful because He is the way, the truth, and the light.

CHAPTER 7

Deborah for such a time

God calling her during a very difficult time is an indicator that He had confidence in her. Deborah is no more special than you or I, just like He called her in a difficult time…He called you or is calling you and I during difficult times. You must be confident in your leadership abilities and in the sovereignty of the One who called you. In this chapter, I want to only focus on how Deborah maximized God's call.

Let's look at Judges 4:4-7:

"4 Now Deborah, a prophet, the wife of Lappidoth, was leading[a] Israel at that time. 5 She held court under the Palm of Deborah between Ramah and Bethel in the hill country of Ephraim, and the Israelites went up to her to have their disputes decided. 6 She sent for Barak son of Abinoam from Kedesh in Naphtali and said to him, 'The Lord, the God of Israel, commands you: "Go, take with you ten thousand men of Naphtali and Zebulun and lead them up to Mount Tabor. 7 I will lead Sisera, the commander of Jabin's army, with his chariots and his troops to the Kishon River and give him into your hands."'"

From Deborah's story we see how to get ready for God to move in our lives and use us an instruments for his glory. Three things we see from her and why she was ready to be used:

#1 She was in position

Deborah was used "for such a time as this" because she was in position to be used. Verse 4 says she was a prophet, a wife, and already leading Israel at the time. Many of us miss God's greater call on our lives because we move out of position because we don't see it moving in the direction we thought it should go. We get convinced that we know the plan that God has and even play that plan over and over in our head and get fixed on what we believe. I'm guilty of it myself but a word of caution, just because you have a plan doesn't mean it's God's plan. I believe one of the reasons Deborah was used for such a time as this is because she was in position and in her lane. In Judges 4:4-5 we see Deborah going about her day as usual. She was posted up in her usual location and doing the work she was assigned to do and then a word from the Lord came forth that would change the course of not just her story but the story of the entire Israelite community. I often counsel and coach people on what to do when you don't know what to do. My advice to them is to do four things

#1 keep going

#2 keep praying

#3 keep watching

#4 keep the faith.

At some point God will speak concerning your situation. Many times, I have found that He speaks when we are doing our everyday task. I can't tell you how many times He has spoken when I'm doing dishes or watching a movie. It's what we do prior to Him speaking the leaves the doors open for God to speak and move as He sees fit. So, the first thing we see her doing while God moved her toward "such a time as this" is she simply keeps doing what she was assigned to do.

#2 She's not afraid

She held the position of judge and became a trusted woman of faith. There is no way to be a great military leader without first being a wise person. Again, she was in a position for greatness. We don't see her veering off into what she thought she should do. We don't see her looking at what another leader was doing she seems to be very content in her role and she is executing where God has placed her. She says to Barak (in essence), "Here's what God has told you to do. I'm going to do my part to be certain you are successful; however, you have to do your part so that comprehensively what God wants will come to pass." This is a woman moving out of just judging into prophetically speaking to a man and telling him what to do based on her time in prayer with God. It's extremely uncommon to hear a woman leading in this way, yet she is doing it. She was not afraid to move out of what seems to be her role as judge into her role as prophetess. She is ready because she knows that her time in prayer was not in vain. God spoke to her at some point concerning the situation and in due time we see her releasing what God spoke "for such a time as this" so the circumstances of the Israelites would change. It didn't just happen…she put her time in to be used by God and that's the message I want you to leave this chapter understanding. It's not just getting up singing a song or preparing a sermon or praying like you've done year after year but it's about putting in the daily work for God to speak to you. As He speaks then you speak out what He gave you, or you sing out what He gave you, or you pray out what He gave you. The point is you must put in the work. The spiritual work necessary so your "for such a time as this" season will come and alter somebody's life for the better.

#3 She was ready for elevation.

Just like anything else in life, when you are doing a good job at some point you can expect to be elevated, which is what happened to Deborah. We see her moving from a judge in Israel to now walking in the prophetic when she tells Barak a word from the Lord, which was to go and wage war against Sisera and his army. If you want to be used by God then you have to be in position, you have to work where you are planted and then you have to move in elevation. We don't see her accusing God of having the wrong vessel as we see in the story of Moses, we see her just going with God's flow. This theme "for such a time as this" is made famous by the story of Esther. Esther is another amazing woman of faith that God elevated in due time. She was beautiful and used her beauty righteously to get ahead. Once she became a queen she prayed and fasted and saved her people from annihilation. Deborah is doing the same thing. She is using what God gave her to achieve God's will in her life and what she can accomplish in her life will help, bless, and even give life to somebody else. We don't accomplish God's will only for us. We do it ultimately for somebody else. It's never all about you. We do what we do for God out of obedience, but it's always going to bless somebody else. If what you are doing for God is only benefiting you then it more than likely is not something from God. Everything we do for God is for somebody else. We may benefit as well but it will always bless somebody else in the long run.

#4 She didn't look at the impossible

Here's the part that I love about Deborah's story. She didn't look at the impossible. Let's look at Judges 4:2-3, "² So the Lord sold them into the hands of Jabin king of Canaan, who reigned in Hazor. Sisera, the commander of his army, was based in Harosheth Haggoyim. ³ Because he had nine hundred chariots fitted with iron and had cruelly oppressed the Israelites for twenty years, they cried to the Lord for help." Here's what she was facing:

- 20 years of oppression
- 900 chariots fitted with iron.
- She was a woman.

Let's dive in:

20 Years of anything is a long time. If you do anything for 20 years and then try to go in a different direction, you're going to find it very difficult to do. Although the Israelites wanted to be free, there still would be a lot of breaking, shifting, movement

to get them free from the hand of their enemies. For now, her focus was to physically get them free, and God would have to deal with the rest. God used her and others to systemically break the bondage of 20 years of oppression. That's a lot of faith that God had in her. The next thing she was facing was 900 chariots fitted with iron. The reason the Israelites were in such trouble and now facing an impossible enemy with iron chariots is because they failed to do what God had original told them to do. They were originally told to eradicate the Canaanites from the earth. None were supposed to live. Now, some say that it meant to eradicate the dark, evil, and demonic practices of the Canaanites while others say it meant to literally kill them all. The truth is, I can see both points here. Sometimes things need to just die, no ifs ands or buts. You don't cut out a portion of cancer, you cut it all out. None of it can remain or the chances of it coming back in full force is highly likely. On the other hand, if you have stomach problems, you don't cut out the whole stomach, you find out what is causing it and you solve for it through medication, surgery, or whatever is causing the issue. So, I don't know what God was looking to do exactly, but what I do know is he wanted the demonic things the Canaanites were doing to stop on sight. But as the story goes it did not stop and now 20 years later the Israelites are dealing with the consequences. The thing they were supposed to kill was left to live and was able to gain power. Now they have to figure out how to overpower something that has grown stronger with every passing year. I want to practically paint this picture. If you and I have a strong hold in our life that we know needs to be removed, how do we know it needs to be removed? The scriptures will tell us. If we know it needs to be removed and we do nothing to remove it, every year that we allow it to remain it will get stronger and stronger. At some point it will grow to the point and place that it will seem impossible to destroy. When something seems impossible to destroy or remove from our lives, we typically will allow it to remain and justify why it's there. Let me give you some examples. If you are addicted to smoking, you know God's word tells us that our bodies are temples of the Holy Spirit and that we should not abuse our temples with the many smoke choices of the day. We do it anyway and we justify it by saying "this keeps me calm, or this is better than taking pills to control my anxiety." We justify instead of eradicating. We leave it as a part of our lives because it has become a part of our lives. It is something we do every day so it's a part of our lives. My bed is a part of my life, my pillows are a part of my life, my favorite workout pants are a part of my life because these are things that I use consistently. If you don't believe me, remove my favorite pillow from my bed, I will notice that it's not my pillow. Put me in a motel for the night. I will know that's not my bed. You get my point. Something that is a part of our lives is going to be hard to remove. That's why we can't allow sin to be a part of our lives. When we recognize it...we need to remove it. It can't stay, it must go. Going back to how this ties into Deborah, she now has to eradicate something that should have been dead a long time ago. Then lastly, she is a woman. As much as we don't want to focus on that fact, it is a fact. She has to do what typically men are called to do. She has to do it with the same authority and the same power. I couldn't image the struggles she went through because her reign was during a time when women were treated as second class citizens. I'm a woman in modern day times and it's a struggle for me to step into spaces that typically men dominate, so I couldn't imagine her doing the same during that time. The point here is "it was for such a time as this." I don't think she even focused on the fact that she was a woman. She did note it to Barak but didn't seem to focus on it. Deborah seemed to be focused on the task at hand and knew that God called her for a specific purpose and a specific time. That's what I want to say to you today my dear sister in Christ. God has called you to THIS

PLACE, for THIS TIME, for THIS PURPOSE. You fill in the place and purpose but if you're reading this right now it is highly likely it's for THIS TIME. So, let's move...right now, "for such a time as this."

CHAPTER 8

Deborah and the Apostle Paul

Well, let's deal with it (smile). The Apostle Paul is the man who wrote 2/3rds of the New Testament. He is an inspiration to all people of God. He is the poster child for what Christianity is supposed to look like. He was at war with God through God's people. He beat, killed, and scattered God's people. But, one day, that all changed on the Damascus road. It was on that road that Paul who was already spiritually blind became physically blind but through his encounter with God he was set up to be one of the greatest ambassadors Christianity has ever seen. I'm very impressed with Paul, however, there are some things that have confused me over the years and this may be the chapter to help me and you settle a few things as it relates to the things that Paul has said specifically about women.

Read Ephesians 5:22-23. Do women really need to submit to their husband IN ALL THINGS? If so, what does that mean? Is this relevant in the world of today because things have changed so much? I mean in those days men did the working and wives took care of the home and the family. That doesn't seem to be the norm anymore, so is this direction out of date? Here's another one I'm confused about, 1 Corinthians 14:34. Do women really need to remain silent in churches? If so, does that mean we can't talk or just can't preach and teach? That same scripture goes on to say, "as the law says." Are we still under law or grace? What about the next verse? Verse 35 says "If they want to inquire about something, they should ask their own husbands at home; for it is disgraceful for a woman to speak in the church." What if they don't have a husband? I don't have one, what am I going to do? Most people I've spoken to would disagree with this text, claiming it's not relevant for today. I agree this scripture is not relevant for today, but if we don't hold women to this standard how do we hold them to any other standard that Paul seems to put forth in regard to women? In 1 Timothy 2:11-15 Paul says, "I do not permit women to speak in church," so is that his preference or should all pastors follow this standard? Lastly, are we following all things Paul said to all people or just the things that keep women in a box? Yikes! Let's jump into it!!!

Do women really need to submit to their husband IN ALL THINGS?

The answer is yes; however, it's not as simple as you think. Women should submit to their husbands, but this shouldn't be a burden but a pleasure. In my life of dating, I have noticed that it's pretty easy to submit to a man that understands that submission doesn't mean subordination. Submissive means we have decided as a couple to do things God's way. It starts with a husband being submitted to God and once he is submitted to God and handling his authority scripturally a women will naturally submit. I remember speaking to a man who believed men had authority over their wives but the harmony in the relationship started with her respecting him, THEN he'd love her as Christ loved the church. I asked him how could that be possible if the husband is the leader? I mean, doesn't it always start with the leader? I am a bi-vocational preacher and where I work it starts with me because I'm the leader. I set the tone for the day and I'm directly or even indirectly in charge of what goes right and wrong throughout that day. It would be considered failed leadership to put responsibility that clearly is for me to manage on the associates. I'm in charge, I signed up for it, I take responsibility for it. I don't get to tell the associates, "When you respect me then I'll lead you." No, I lead and manage them no matter how they treat me, THEN the expectation is for them to follow. It doesn't start with them...it starts with me. So, the same holds true in a marriage. Love starts with the husband and respect follows from the wife. Leadership is not secondary...it is primary. So yes, a wife should follow her husband in all things as he follows AND LEADS. PLEASE NOTE, if you can't respect him, don't marry him. PLEASE NOTE AGAIN, if you can't love her AS CHRIST LOVES THE CHURCH, don't marry her. So yes, a wife should follow **HER OWN** husband in all things. Note I put in bold letters and all caps **HER OWN** husband, because she should reserve this level of respect and honor for her husband, not her boyfriend.

Since things have changed so much is submission practical?

Submission is practical. Things have certainly changed, but God and His word will never change. But, with that being said, what does submission really look like? Submission means to revere her husband. Which means to respect and admire him greatly. Let me give you a little tip. You should marry a man that you can respect. I have found that respect comes very easy for me when a man provides a safe place for my femininity to flourish. If I'm going to be honest though, I have dated men that I struggle to respect and it wasn't because they were not respectable, it was all in my head. So, let me give you some advice on how to respect a respectable man when you're in your own head. For clarification "being in your own head" would be that he's a respectable man but does things that you don't respect. I'm confusing myself, so let me give you a list of what I mean.

- He's a respectable man but has no vision.
- He's a respectable man but has no drive.

- He's a respectable man but has no self-awareness.
- He's a respectable man but wants to control you.
- He's a respectable man but gives credence to his own call and none to your call.

Here's some tips on how to respect a respectable man who does things that make you want to disrespect him:

Respect what they do:

It is easy to respect an affluent man. I mean after all he is somebody. If he's a lawyer, doctor, preacher, pastor, or anything that represents power it is easy to respect him. The fact is most men we meet on a daily basis will not be a doctor, lawyer, preacher, or pastor; some (most) will just be regular Joe's... now what? You may be saying I can't respect a janitor or a supervisor at *Chick-Fil-A*, and I totally get it, but can you respect what they do for you? Meaning maybe they can't buy you an expensive piece of jewelry or maybe all they can do is buy you a purse from Target, but does he treat you right? Does he love you right? Does he build you up and not tear you down? If the answer is yes, then you'd do yourself a huge favor to learn to work with him. You are respecting what he does for you, not necessarily what he does for a living. I guess the picture I'm trying to paint is respect what you can respect even if you have to think long and hard about it. Find it and let that be your starting point for respecting him.

Respect who they are

Again, as stated above, you and I may not find a lawyer or a doctor. We may find an everyday Joe, but you can respect who they are. If you marry a man of God (and you should) then you can learn to appreciate him as such. If he attends church on a regular basis, prays consistently, listens, and guides you in truth through the word of God you should hold on for dear life and throw a parade in his honor (lol). Seriously, these types of men are a rarity now a days so you should definitely learn to respect the God in him. Well, Dr. Juanita, what if he's not doing all of that but he's a good man who loves God and loves me? What then? Respect him, love him, and build a life with him because you may just be Deborah and he may Lappidoth.

Respect their commitment to something or somebody

But what if your average Joe is a Christian but not able to lead you spiritually? Then respect their commitment to you, your marriage, your children, his God or maybe something he does that gives back to a group or a community.

The point here is men NEED respect. I don't know about you, but I've heard this my entire life, but nobody tells us how to respect or how to process through respect. I've found that many women want to respect but they aren't always aware of how to process through respect, especially in a day when respect seems to be given based on assets and money and not for the simple and small things. Since most of us will marry or are already married to average Joes I think articulating how to submit to them through respect is vitally important.

Do women really need to remain silent at church?

Nope! Cue next chapter (lol). No, but the answer is no. Women are allowed to speak in the church. Here is the context:

> *"Women should remain silent in the churches.*
> *They are not allowed to speak, but must be in sub-*
> *mission, as the law says"* (1 Corinthians 14:34).

The issue is not that women should not talk at church. How do we know that? Because just before 1 Corinthians 14 and 34 Paul gives instruction on Men and WOMEN prophesying at church in 1 Corinthians 11:4-5.

"⁴ Every man who prays or prophesies with his head covered dishonors his head. ⁵ But every woman who prays or prophesies with her head uncovered dishonors her head—it is the same as having her head shaved" (1 Corinthians 11:4-5).

So, if women are not supposed to speak in church, how in the world would they prophesy? Last time I checked people don't prophesy in silence. So, that couldn't be what Paul meant. 1 Corinthians 14:34 boils down to women chattering to much during service and causing distractions. He's saying to the women, in essence, "stop all the extra talk during service because you're disrupting the house." He goes on and gives them the answer to their next question (before they even ask) and instructs them that if the chattering is coming from confusion about what is being taught then talk to your husband but do it once you get home. I think Paul knew that some women would justify the chatter by saying they were asking questions from some of the other women about the service or what was being taught in the service. The point is Paul nor God expects women to not speak in the church. Okay, so that takes care of the married women but what about the unmarried women? Who helps us? Well, the answer is we help ourselves through our own relationship with God, our pastor, and other means to understand the Bible and God's expectations of us through women's groups, Bible study and/or conferences and church services.

Can women preach in the church?
The answer is yes (see the scriptures below)
"He had four unmarried daughters who prophesied" (Acts 21:9).

Philippians 4:2-3
I plead with Euodia and I plead with Syntyche to be of the same mind in the Lord. ³ Yes, and I ask you, my true companion, help these women since they have contended at my side in

the cause of the gospel, along with Clement and the rest of my co-workers, whose names are in the book of life.

Titus 2:3-5

[3] Likewise, teach the older women to be reverent in the way they live, not to be slanderers or addicted to much wine, but to teach what is good. [4] Then they can urge the younger women to love their husbands and children, [5] to be self-controlled and pure, to be busy at home, to be kind, and to be subject to their husbands, so that no one will malign the word of God.

Luke 2:36-38

[36] There was also a prophet, Anna, the daughter of Penuel, of the tribe of Asher. She was very old; she had lived with her husband seven years after her marriage, [37] and then was a widow until she was eighty-four.[a] She never left the temple but worshiped night and day, fasting and praying.[38] Coming up to them at that very moment, she gave thanks to God and spoke about the child to all who were looking forward to the redemption of Jerusalem.

1 Corinthians 11:5

[5] But every woman who prays or prophesies with her head uncovered dishonors her head—it is the same as having her head shaved.

Can women pastor in the church?

The answer depends on how you look at the scriptures (see below).

Mark 16:15

[15] *He said to them, "Go into all the world and preach the gospel to all creation.*

When you preach the gospel, and it is not gender specific on who teaches who, then there could very well be space to interpret this scripture as saying a woman can teach a man.

Acts 2:17-18

"'In the last days, God says,
I will pour out my Spirit on all people.
Your sons and daughters will prophesy,
your young men will see visions,
your old men will dream dreams.
18 Even on my servants, both men and women,
I will pour out my Spirit in those days,
and they will prophesy.

In the last day. I don't know about any of you, but I believe we are closer to the end than ever before. I'm not saying that will happen tomorrow, but I do believe He's on His way back. Could that explain the rise in women preachers and pastors? I don't know, but what I do know is there is definitely a rise of women moving into lead pastor roles in the church and we definitely seem to be living in the last days.

1 Corinthians 11:4-6

4 Every man who prays or prophesies with his head covered dishonors his head. 5 But every woman who prays or prophesies with her head uncovered dishonors her head—it is the same as having her head shaved. 6 For if a woman does not cover her head, she might as well have her hair cut off; but if it is a disgrace for a woman to have her hair cut off or her head shaved, then she should cover her head.

As noted in this book, already there are different types of prophets or prophetess. A pastor is definitely a prophet as he or she forthtells the word of God.

According to Paul, was Deborah aligned with scripture? I believe that she was as her responsibility was to be a judge over Israel and to prophesy or forthtell what God wanted Barak to do. She did exercise authority over Barak as she told him what God told her. Now, some may think I'm stretching this a little bit but isn't that what pastor's do week after week? Don't they simply give instructions to the people (men and women alike) and tell them what God has said? I'll leave that there, but I do think God has a history of choosing women to operate in uncommon positions. Look at Deborah, or Esther, even the women at the tomb (Anna and all the Mary's). It is my belief that God is raising up women in the season like we've never seen before and to be honest I don't know why BUT I'm humbled and grateful.

As I close this chapter, I want to humor you but at the same time just put this out there. There are numerous things that the Bible does not permit but we still give a pass on today. This is not to say we should pick and choose what we believe about the word, but it is to say either we are going to follow it completely or we are not. So, here we go...five things that we do that we should not do according to the Bible:

#5 Wear Polyester, Leviticus 19:19
#4 Wear Gold, 1 Timothy 2:9
#3 Eat Shellfish, Leviticus 11:10
#2 Tattoos, Leviticus 19:28
#1 Remarry after divorce, Mark 10:11-12

CHAPTER 9

Deborah and Jael

I have a question. Is anybody sick and tired of the housewives of this and the housewives of that? I personally am sick of it! It is because these types of shows are all centered around women behaving badly for ratings. Now, on one hand these women seem to be living their best lives, but the deeper issue is this type of show impacts the modern-day woman. As much as we don't want to admit we are a world of followers, the fact is, we are and it's really sad. This is why I love Deborah! She is a leader through and through! The day and time that Deborah was in was not a time that women would lead and certainly not lead a nation of people. Deborah told Barak to take ten thousand men and lead them up to Mount Tabor. She said she would lead Sisera and his chariots and troops to the Kishon River and give him over to Barak. Barak told her only if she would go with him would he do it. Deborah agreed but prophesied and told him because of his stance that the victory would go to a woman. Now, if you stopped reading there you'd think she would naturally mean herself, but Deborah didn't mean herself she meant Jael. Unlike the world that we live in today, this is not a girl behaving poorly to get her name out there or a woman behaving in a way to get attention for herself and get attention off of another woman. This is a Godly woman. A woman who prioritizes the things of God and His plan over her plan. She knew that she was just a part of the story. She was not the story! I love this! I wish we had more of it in modern day society. Something interesting to note, Jael and her people were not at war with Sisera and the Canaanites; Jael was a Kenite. That's why Sisera felt comfortable hiding in her tent. Let's read how these two unlikely people met.

Judges 4:14-18 says:

> *¹⁴ Then Deborah said to Barak, "Go! This is the day the Lord has given Sisera into your hands. Has not the Lord gone ahead of you?" So Barak went down Mount Tabor, with ten thousand men following him. ¹⁵ At Barak's advance, the Lord routed Sisera and all his chariots and army by the sword, and Sisera got down from his chariot and fled on foot.*

> *¹⁶ Barak pursued the chariots and army as far as Harosheth Haggoyim, and all Sisera's troops fell by the sword; not a man was left. ¹⁷ Sisera, meanwhile, fled on foot to the tent of Jael, the wife of Heber the Kenite, because there was an alliance between Jabin king of Hazor and the family of Heber the Kenite.*

> *¹⁸ Jael went out to meet Sisera and said to him, "Come, my lord, come right in. Don't be afraid." So, he entered her tent, and she covered him with a blanket.*

We can certainly learn a lot from her although we don't know much about her. All we know is she was a Bedouin *(indigenous people of the Negev desert in southern Israel)* and a wife. Her husband was Heber the Kenite. We also know her name means "Mountain Goat." Which is fitting because a mountain goat is not actually a goat, they are more like gazelles or cattle. Jael appeared to be a woman that would help Sisera but turned out to be the woman who would take his life. They are very aggressive, which is like

Jael who put a peg through Sisera's head when given the opportunity. But I digress, there are many lessons we can learn from her. Below are just a few:

#1 She acted when opportunity presented itself

As mentioned earlier, she nor her people were enemies with the Canaanites so there was no real reason to kill Sisera. The Kenites were friendly with the Israelites but there was no alliance between the two tribes. I think it's relatively easy to answer why Jael killed Sisera.

A. She acted on the opportunity as it was presented to her, but I also think it was divine design. Deborah, you'll remember, already spoke prophetically that the credit for the victory would not go to Barak but to a woman. She never said she would get the credit but she simply said a woman would. I believe it was God who led Sisera to that tent and it was God who inclined Jael to drive the tent peg into Sisera's head, giving the Israelites the upper hand and eventually the victory over the Canaanites. The point here is God wants to move in our lives, but we have to be ready when He gives the unction. The old saying is to "strike while the iron is hot."

#2 She used what she had

I love the word! I love teaching the word. I'm not the best speaker or teacher but I use what I have. Some may love it, and some may not, but really none of that matters because I'm using what I believe God gave me. All Jael had was a tent peg, a mission, and an utterance from God. She took what she had and used it to give the Israelites victory. One of the things I love about God is how He will take what little we have and make much. He will take a big problem with little resources and work miracles. I absolutely love the math of God. He can take two and multiply it by six then minus it by four and you still have not lost a thing. Everything balances out in the math of God.

#3 She said yes to God and no to cultural norms.

We are in a world that the line of the Christian walk and the cultural norms are so blurred that we can't always tell who is a Christian and who is not. I must admit at times it's hard to know who is a Christian and who is not. We all just seem to be in a big chef salad that's tossed and mixed altogether. That's not the way it should be. God has called us out of darkness. He's called us to not blend but to be bold. There should be a difference between the Christian and the world. We see in the life of Jael a woman who is clearly standing on the right side of history, although some would say she broke rules that should have never been broken, like inviting a man to her tent. She was not hospitable like she should have been, I mean after all she gave him milk when he asked for water probably to help him doze off to sleep so she could then attack him. She also undermined her husband because he was at peace with King Jabin, probably because the Kenites were metal workers and probably repaired and made weapons for the king and his people. See Judges 4:17, *"17 Sisera, meanwhile, fled on foot to the tent of Jael, the wife of Heber the Kenite, because there was an alliance between Jabin king of Hazor and the family of Heber the Kenite."*

We don't see that she ever consulted with her husband about anything. She just saw the opportunity and took it. While none of these things are necessarily correct, we do see her following in the steps of Jesus when He challenged cultural norms for the kingdom. We see Jesus challenging cultural norms by:

- Denouncing leaders who put too much pressure on the people (Matthew 23)
- Touching leapers although He wasn't supposed to (Matthew 8:3)
- Healing on the sabbath (Mark 3:1-6)

Although I'm not advocating undermining anybody in authority over you, I do believe we need to walk like Jesus did. Jesus made a clear distinction between Himself and those who were not of God. He didn't do it from a place of being better than anybody else. He did it from the place of separating Himself out because He understood the call that was on His life. We as women of faith should understand the call that is on our lives and be sure we separate ourselves out of darkness as well.

#4 She honored God

This should be our stance as believers in Christ. Our stance should be clear, and that is to honor God. Again, as I said earlier, I think it's easy to get lost in the sauce because we have so much going on in the world we are in. We get up and go hard every day to earn a living. We have church activities, we have children's activities, we have marriage responsibilities. It can be very overwhelming, but we have to learn to put God first. When we put God first, we honor Him. When we honor Him and put Him first, we will be able to clearly see when He is moving and when He is speaking. Remember, Jael was nowhere around when Deborah spoke prophetically that a woman would get the credit for the victory. She had to be putting God first by honoring Him above and beyond everything. How else could she hear Him telling her to kill Sisera, which would be getting the Israelites one step closer to victory? That's what we need to learn to do even though we are busy in life. We have to learn to honor God, so we are ready to move when He moves or when He moves us.

#5 She teaches us how to fight in the spiritual

Although I'm sure she didn't know it at the time, she gives us a glimpse of how to fight our spiritual battles. Charles Spurgeon in one of his famous sermon's compared sin to Sisera. He said that we should see sin and then pursue it, then kill it like Jael did him. I'd say it this way, we should pursue sin not to emerge in it but to eradicate it from our lives. We ought to see sin, identify it as the enemy, similar to what Jael did, then stick a peg through its ugly head. We ought to hate sin and the power of darkness that brought it to our door. Jael teaches us that evil is not to be played with. It has to be dealt with. Do you have any sin in your life? You need to deal with it. If you don't know if you have sin in your life then I'd challenge you before you turn another page in this book for you to ask God to help you identify it, repent, and then ask God for a plan of escape against it. Deborah and Jael are two unlikely, ordinary women who were determined to do right by God and because of that they were able to defeat an army that stood in the way of God's people going to the next level in Him. I bet you feel like an ordinary woman too, but remember God can do more for us ordinary women as long as we have a heart and mind that's yielded to His will over our will.

CHAPTER 10

Deborah and you

Well, we made it to the end of the book. I first want to thank you for reading the book and my prayer is that you will utilize every word written to become what God has called you to be. We've learned so much about Deborah and her contribution to both Jewish and Christian history. I wanted to end the book with just a few more things that I think we can learn from Deborah and hopefully you will apply these last few lessons to your walk.

Glorifying God is always in season.

As we know, this walk will produce some highs as well as some lows. In times of great struggle there is a tendency for the believer to forget about God. Why? Because when everything is going great there is a tendency to forget to be grateful. The problem with being in a good place is that at some point we will come down from the high place and be back in the valley low. When we go into the valley low, we typically are in great need for God's help, but we've lost too much ground in the high and ungrateful moments of life. The Israelites, like many of us, seem to only focus on God while they are in trouble.... but it gets worse. To make matters worse, they allow idolatry and sin to enter into their culture which further separates them from right standing with God. The Israelites bought into the lies of the enemy by thinking they could serve two masters, sin and God, which they cannot, nor can we. When we allow ourselves to become compromised we become prey to the enemy and his tactics. One lesson we learn from Deborah is our walk with Christ must be a walk of continuous seeking, continuous serving, continuous pruning, least we become prey to the enemy. How would I best tell you to apply this portion of the book into your personal walk with Jesus Christ? Learn to make your walk a lifestyle, not a diet or a buffet. We need God every day consistently and continually just like we need good nourishment. We don't just need food, we need good food or we will be unhealthy. Christianity is a lifestyle. You must wake up every day with God on your mind. That's how you guard yourself from sin entering into your life. Glorifying God is always in season for the Christian, but how do we put glorifying God into practice? How do we glorify Him as lifestyle? Let me give you 5 ways:

We glorify Him with our mouths.
Psalm 63:3

The psalmist says that loving God is better than life and so because of that God deserves the glorification from our mouths.

We glorify Him by doing what He says through His word
Isaiah 48:17

He teaches us what is right and leads us on the way to go. We glorify Him by listening to His teachings and following His direction through obedience.

Pray in Jesus Name
Romans 6:23

For the wages of sin is death but the gift of God is eternal life.

When we pray, we pray in Jesus' name because He is the promise of blessings in our life, first and foremost, but we pray in His name because He is the only reason that we have access to God. We pray in His name because His name has authority that He has graciously afforded to us to fight off the devil, calm the storms of life, and give us peace that passes all understanding and that is only made possible in His name.

Produce good spiritual food

John 15:8

"My Father is glorified by this: that you produce much fruit and prove to be my disciples."

Just like a fruit tree is expected to bear good fruit, so is the Christian. We don't expect a tree just to bear fruit but if they are going to be useful we expect it to bear good fruit. God didn't pull us out to bear rotten fruit but good fruit showing who He is. Whether we like it or not we represent Christ. Everything we do when we become a follower of Christ represents Him. So, when we produce good fruit, when we show the onlookers that we serve God in more than words but in actions and sacrifice, we honor God and give them a clear picture of what being a Christian looks like.

Live Lives Worthy of Redemption

1 Peter 2:12

"Conduct yourselves honorably among the Gentiles, so that when they slander you as evildoers, they will observe your good works and will glorify God on the day he visits."

You were redeemed for a reason. Don't forget that. Your redemption was not to just send you to heaven, but your redemption was for you to pull someone else out and for them to do the same. We are put on the earth for a spiritual purpose and, believe it or not, it is not only about you. That sounds harsh but it's true. We are now in a world where we are under intense pressure to be pretentious. We are told in so many words to make it about us. We hear things like "self-care," or "preserving my peace," but the truth is the real translation is "prioritize yourself over and above anything else." I must admit that I fell into that trap. I bought into the "I've raised my children; I've sacrificed enough and now it's all about me," but to be honest with you it never felt right. It never felt right because it wasn't right. We are called to live lives that are worthy of redemption. What does that life look like? It's to put God first in everything and watch everything you need be added to you. God is not a man that He should lie (Number 23:19). He tells us in His Word the recipe to abundant life, which is to put Him first (Matthew 6:33). I'm learning everyday how this truth works. I will tell you that I'm at my happiest when I do put Him first and I'm at my saddest when I don't. Deborah understood this. She had to. She put God first and everything else worked itself out. She was great for God, and I believe that had to be because of this heavenly principle. I said earlier that the Christian lifestyle could not be a buffet or a diet, meaning we can't do it in small doses because we won't be healthy. Have you ever seen a person who ate very little? They consumed so few calories that over time they weren't just skinny, they looked sick. That's what happens when we don't eat enough spiritual food. In that same vein, being a Christian shouldn't have us eating it like we are at a buffet. What does that mean? It means eating so much of it that we become so heavy that nobody can pick us up because we have an inflated ego that can't fit into a room. We've all seen people who are so heaven bound that they are no earthly good. They are unrelatable, judgmental, and of no service to the people of God. The right recipe for Christianity is we have to have the right ingredients, make time to prepare the meal, set a beautiful table, and then plate out that which was prepared and consume the spiritual food for use in the Kingdom. It's a process but a worthy process and a valuable process. Deborah really impressed me and I truly felt lead by God to write about her. Her story came to me while talking to God about a relationship I was in at the time. In this relationship I was misunderstood. I was treated poorly and blamed for standing up for myself. I remember talking to God and explaining to Him, well actually pleading with Him, for my love interest to just understand that I had a Deborah spirit on me. I said "God, why can't he just understand that I AM DEB-

ORAH?" and although I was on a ten, God was not. He simply said "Yes, you are, now what are you going to do about it?" It was at that exact moment that I Am Deborah was born, and a year later we are here. I allowed Deborah's story to encourage me and I hope that you will do the same. You have Deborah on the inside of you or you probably wouldn't have made it to the end of this book. I challenge you to be bold like Deborah, say "what thus saith the Lord" like Deborah. Challenge societal norms like Deborah and change the world like Deborah.

ENDNOTES

1 Apolitical. "Women Belong in All Places Where Decisions Are Being Made." Accessed July 6, 2023. https://apolitical.co/solution-articles/en/women-belong-in-all-places-where-decisions-are-being-made.

2 Maeterlinck, Maurice. "The Life of the Bee." *Project Gutenburg*. Accessed July 6, 2023. https://www.gutenberg.org/ebooks/4511/pg4511-images.html.utf8.

Printed in the USA
CPSIA information can be obtained
at www.ICGtesting.com
JSHW010514250124
55700JS00011B/118